Unstuck: Brutal Guidance for Getting Out of Your Own Way

Philip Huffman

Copyright

Unstuck: Brutal Guidance for Getting Out of Your Own Way
by Philip Huffman
Copyright ©2025 by Philip Huffman. All rights reserved.
No part of this book may be reproduced, stored in a retrieval system, or transmitted in any form or by any means, electronic, mechanical, photocopying, recording, or otherwise without prior written permission from the author, except for brief quotes in reviews or articles. This book is provided for informational purposes only. The author makes no representations or warranties regarding the accuracy or applicability of the content. The reader assumes full responsibility for their actions based on this material.
For permissions or inquiries, contact: Philip.R.Huffman@gmail.com

ISBN

ePub:	979-8-9926021-0-4
Ingram Spark Hardcover:	979-8-9926021-2-8
KDP Hardcover:	979-8-9926021-4-2
KDP Paperback:	979-8-9926021-1-1

Version 1.1 – April 2025
Published by PRH

Dedication

To those warriors who chose action.

Epigraph

"It's not enough to choose what matters. If you want your values to make a difference in your life, you also have to act on them."

Steven C. Hayes, *The Subtle Art of Doing What Matters*

Contents

Dedication   v

Epigraph   vii

Contents   ix

Foreword   xi

Preface   xv

1   Stop Stalling   1

2   Your Excuses Are BS   7

3   Embrace Discomfort   13

4   Don't Negotiate with Yourself   19

5   Action Comes First   25

6   Stack Wins   31

7   Persistence Over Perfection   37

8   Don't Miss Twice   45

Afterword   51

About the Author	55
From the Author	61
Acknowledgments	63
Key Principles	64
Reading List	65
30-Day Momentum Challenge	69
Prompts for Chapter Illustrations	73
Notes	77

Foreword

Any educator will tell you that although we meet thousands of students in our careers, a handful just stick with us, whether we have them for one semester or four. I met Phil Huffman in the fall of 2010. I was teaching U.S. History since 1865. I'd been a full-time history instructor for 3 years, and I still had a lot to learn. Phil is a student who made me a better teacher.

He was impossible not to notice. In a room full of teen- and twenty-somethings, in the front row sat this huge, bearded, 50-something veteran. From the first day, I knew this was someone special. It wasn't just the active spark of intellect and curiosity in his eyes; it was his willingness to challenge and engage me and his fellow students. Phil asked questions, but he also contributed his own knowledge and experiences with humility and kindness even when he was correcting me. I learned quickly in our conversations after class that Phil, like me, was a U.S. Army veteran, that this was a proud part of his biography, but not an uncomplicated one. We talked about the challenges of reintegrating into civilian life after serving, and I sensed that for Phil, this had been a rockier process than for me, a Gulf War era vet at least 15 years his junior.

Phil reached out to me several times after he'd moved on from college (having gotten the highest grade in the class, of course). We touched base over political issues and connected on social media, and sometimes I gave him rides to appointments at the VA. Although his good humor was unflagging, I could sense there were struggles in his personal life, and now that I've read his wonderful book, I wish I had been bold enough to ask him more questions. Fortunately, he found the help he needed, not only through therapy, but through his own relentless pursuit of wisdom. A man who quotes Carl Sagan and Ayn Rand in the same volume has clearly been diverse in his quest for truth. Phil is a born philosopher.

It gives me great pleasure to write this foreword, not only because I am honored to have been chosen by Phil, but because this book represents a victory of sorts. We have all struggled, and we have all made excuses for why we can't move forward. Phil shares with us the power of persistence, of personal advocacy, and the quiet magic of taking small steps. The classical philosophers he treasures would recognize him as one of their ideological descendants, a seeker who never stops asking questions and who fundamentally believes that truth is there to be found, if only we have the courage, perseverance, and relentless optimism

to keep looking. I wish Phil well on his continuing journey, and am deeply gratified he has asked me to be a part of it.
Diane A. Boldt
History Instructor
MCC-Longview

Preface

THIS book is not for the faint of heart. It isn't a gentle guide to self-improvement or a collection of feel-good affirmations. It's a wake-up call—a challenge, a demand for action, a kick in the ass.

Too many people shuffle through life waiting for the perfect moment, the perfect opportunity, the perfect conditions to finally start living. But the harsh truth is, there is no perfect moment. There is only now.

This book exists to shake you out of complacency. It will push you to take control, own your decisions, and stop making excuses. The world doesn't owe you success, happiness, or fulfillment. Those are things you have to fight for—things you must create for yourself.

As you turn these pages, be prepared to confront uncomfortable truths. Growth doesn't happen in comfort. It happens when you challenge yourself, push through resistance, and embrace discomfort as the price of progress.

You are not a victim of circumstance. You are the architect of your future. I didn't write this book because I had all the answers—I wrote it because I know what it feels like to be stuck: mentally, emotionally, spiritually. I've lived in that fog where nothing moves, where every decision feels heavy, and even the smallest step seems impossible. Maybe you've been there too.

Unstuck isn't a book of lofty theories. It's not about motivation hacks or catchy slogans. It's about getting out of your own way, even when you don't feel ready. It's about action—real, imperfect, forward-moving action—and the discipline to keep showing up when quitting feels easier.

There's a turning point in every life when excuses become unbearable. When the cost of staying stuck outweighs the fear of moving forward. This book is for that moment. For those who are tired of waiting, tired of trying to think their way out of ruts they can only move through. I'm not offering shortcuts or promises of instant change. What I'm offering is something more durable: a way to build momentum, reclaim your self-respect, and take radical responsibility for the direction of your life.

You won't find perfection in these pages. You'll find principles—hard-earned, tested, and lived. You'll find stories of struggle. And more importantly, what it means to keep going anyway.

If you're holding this book, you've already taken the first step.

Let's take the next one together.

Right now.

1
Stop Stalling

You Have Decisions to Make

"Between stimulus and response there is a space. In that space is our power to choose our response. In our response lies our growth and our freedom."

Viktor Frankl, *Man's Search for Meaning*

We all put our pants on one leg at a time. Some start with the left, some with the right. But guess what? It doesn't matter. At the end of the day, your pants are on, and you're out the door.

People love to think they're special—different, exceptional. And in some ways, they are. No two people are exactly alike. Different backgrounds. Different struggles. Different talents.

But here's the kicker: *everyone* is different. Which, in that respect, makes everyone the same. What matters isn't how unique you are. What matters is what you *do* with it.

Right now, you might be stuck. Spinning your wheels. Waiting for something or someone to change your life. But here's the truth: no one's coming to save you. Your uniqueness? It means nothing if you don't use it.

The world doesn't care about your excuses. It doesn't care about your reasons, your justifications, or your "bad luck." It doesn't hand out participation trophies for trying.

Yes, life is unfair. Yes, bad things happen to good people. But here's the raw truth: whining won't fix a damn thing.

You have two choices:

1. Keep complaining, blaming, and waiting for a miracle.
2. Own your life and start doing something with it.

If you picked the first option, close this book. It's not for you. If you chose the second—good. Let's get to work.

Nobody's saying it's easy. Taking responsibility for your life is hard. It means admitting that a lot of your problems are your fault. *Period.* That's a tough pill to swallow. But once you do, you gain something priceless: *control.*

If your problems are always someone else's fault, you're powerless. You're stuck, just waiting for the universe to fix things. But if you take ownership, you suddenly have the power to change everything.

Hate your job? Find a way out. Unhappy with your body? Change how you eat and move. Stuck in a rut? Stop making excuses and take action. The sooner you stop blaming the world and start owning your life, the sooner things will change.

Forget waiting for motivation. Motivation is unreliable. It comes and goes like a bad Wi-Fi signal. If you rely on motivation, you'll never get anywhere.

The people who succeed aren't the ones who *feel like it* all the time. They're the ones who show up even when they don't. They go to the gym when they'd rather stay in bed. They work on their goals when they're tired. They push forward even when everything sucks. And guess what? That's when the *real* growth happens. When you push through the discomfort, you get stronger.

If you want this book to change your life, don't just read it. *Act* on it.

Right now—yes, RIGHT NOW—I want you to do something that moves you forward. It doesn't have to be huge. Just one action:

- Send that email.
- Take that first step.
- Start that workout.
- Write that first sentence.

Just move. Because movement creates momentum. And momentum? That's what gets you out of your head and into the game of life.

This is your wake-up call. This is your moment.

The question is—are you ready to own your life?

Because nobody's coming to save you. But you? *You can save yourself.*

And it starts right now. Not when you're ready. Not when you feel like it. ***NOW!***

Reflection

- What have you been waiting for before taking action?
- How has that waiting served—or sabotaged—you?
- What's one thing you could do today without waiting to feel "ready"?

Core Message: You must decide how you'll live the rest of your life.

2
Your Excuses Are BS

And You Know It

"We suffer more often in imagination than in reality."

Seneca

P EOPLE don't lack ability—they lack *honesty*.
- They tell themselves stories about why they can't start.
- They create problems that don't exist to justify staying comfortable.
- They confuse reasons with excuses—and it keeps them stuck.
- They mistake planning for progress and never take action.
- They wait to "feel ready" instead of creating momentum.

You say, "I don't have time." The truth is, if you're like most of us, you have time. You just waste it. The hours you squander on Netflix, social media, and doom-scrolling could be put to better use. Track your time. You'll find the gaps. Reclaim your wasted minutes and put them where they matter.

You say, "I don't feel like it." Well, at first, nobody feels like it. If you're waiting for motivation, reread Chapter One. The answer is to commit first—the feelings will follow. Brushing your teeth isn't fun, but you still do it.

You say, "I don't know where to start." Surely there's something—anything—you can do to move in the right direction. Action always beats overthinking. If you're brutally honest, you're not stuck—you're just avoiding the task you need to do. Planning feels productive, but if you never act, it's just procrastination in disguise.

Imagine you're stuck in a huge project. Do you quit? Hell, *NO!* You look at the problem from different angles until something breaks loose. You find a way *forward*.

You say, "I'm not ready, yet." If you wait until you *feel* ready, you might be waiting a very long time. Start now. Clarity comes with action. Young children don't wait until they're ready to walk—they just get up and try. Sure, they fall. At first, they fall a lot. But they get back up, and they get better. Soon—too soon for some—they're running in track meets. Those children just kept going.

Tenacity. That's the answer. Start—stick with it. And *never* quit.

When you catch yourself making an excuse, STOP. Turn that "I can't" into "How *can* I?" Do it immediately. Kill the excuse before it kills your project.

You're either making progress or making excuses. No one's perfect. But the people who win in life? They refuse to let their own B.S. stop them.

You can have results. You can have excuses. You can't have both. This chapter isn't here to make you feel good. It's here to make you honest. To help you stop playing silly games with yourself—and give you a way out. You now know the truth. What, precisely, are you going to do about it?

Put This Into Action:
Write down one truth you've been avoiding. What's one uncomfortable reality you need to face? Identify the next step. Knowing the truth isn't enough –what's one action you can take today based on that truth?
- Commit to action.
- Set a deadline for yourself.
- What will you do, and by when?

Reflection

- How do you currently define discipline?
- What would it look like if you treated discipline as an act of self-respect?
- Where in your life could you use a little more structure?

Core Message: THE QUALITY OF YOUR FUTURE DEPENDS ON THE TRUTHS YOU ARE FACING TODAY.

3
Embrace Discomfort

Get comfortable with being uncomfortable.

"Out of suffering have emerged the strongest souls; the most massive characters are seared with scars."

Khalil Gibran

PAIN need not cause suffering—it can lead to wisdom. Personal growth doesn't come from comfort; it comes from struggle. Every challenge, every setback, every moment of discomfort is an opportunity to build resilience. The people who succeed aren't the ones who avoid pain—they're the ones who face it, own it, and push through anyway.

Yes, you're unique. But what matters isn't how unique you are. What matters is what you *do* with it.

Excuses won't build you. Avoidance won't protect you. Growth is earned, not granted. The only way forward is through—through discomfort, through setbacks, through resistance. You either step up and take control of your life, or you stay exactly where you are. The choice is yours.

Yes, life is unfair. Yes, bad things happen to good people. But here's the raw, unvarnished truth: **whining about it won't fix a damn thing**.

Forget waiting for motivation. Motivation is unreliable. If you rely on motivation, you are *doomed*. Discipline beats motivation every time because discipline doesn't rely on your feelings.

The people who succeed aren't the ones who feel like it every time. They're the ones who show up even when they don't. They go to the gym when they'd rather stay in bed. They work on their goals even when they're tired. They push forward even when things suck. And yes, things *will* suck—sometimes a lot. Guess what? **That's** when the real growth happens. When you push through the discomfort, you get stronger.

Just as discomfort is necessary for growth, toxic people are deadly to momentum. They feed on negativity, doubt, and excuses—and they'll drag you down with them if you let them. Remember, they can't do it without your permission.

Look for these traits to identify toxic people:

- They constantly complain but rarely take action.
- They make you feel guilty for your progress.
- They dismiss your goals as unrealistic or too ambitious.
- They feed into your self-doubt instead of pushing you forward.

When you find yourself spending time with someone toxic, use these tactics to protect your energy:

- **Limit exposure.** Don't give toxic people more of your time than absolutely necessary.

- **Set boundaries.** Be clear about what you will and won't tolerate—and stick to it, with tenacity.
- **Find the right crowd.** Surround yourself with people who push you higher.

Truth Bomb: Jim Rohn said you are the average of the five people you spend the most time with. If those people aren't lifting you up, they're dragging you down. Choose your friends wisely.

Imagine standing at a crossroads, each path representing a choice that could reshape your life. This book is only your guide. You must take that first step. Right now, commit to a single, decisive action:
- Draft that email you've been postponing.
- Lace up and begin that workout.
- Pen the opening line of that project you've been avoiding.

Action ignites momentum, propelling you from contemplation into tangible progress. Embrace the discomfort—it's an indication of growth. The more you challenge yourself, the more resilient you become. No more delays. No more excuses. It's your life. Take charge and move forward.

Put This Into Action:
- Do one thing today that makes you uncomfortable. It could be as small as speaking up in a conversation or as big as tackling a tough project.
- Identify a past challenge. Think of a time when discomfort led to growth.
- Reflect: How did you get through it? Use that memory as proof that you can do it again.

Reflection

- What discomfort have you been avoiding?
- What has avoidance cost you—physically, emotionally, or creatively?
- What's one small discomfort you're willing to face this week?

Core Message: Growth begins at the edge of your comfort zone. Lean into discomfort, and you will find your strength.

4
Don't Negotiate with Yourself

Motivation Is a Big Fat Liar

"It is far better to grasp the universe as it really is than to persist in delusion, however satisfying and reassuring."

Carl Sagan, *The Demon-Haunted World*

MOTIVATION is great—when you have it. But it's fleeting. If you rely on motivation, you'll only take action when you feel like it.

Discipline doesn't care about feelings. The disciplined person accomplishes the mission. No matter what.

Do you actually think successful people wake up feeling motivated every day? They don't. They wake up tired, annoyed, unmotivated—just like you. But they do it anyway. Because they've trained themselves to show up.

Real power comes when you show up on the bad days. When you don't feel like going to the gym—go. When you don't feel like writing—write. When you don't feel like working—do the job, *do it well*.

How to Build Discipline

1. **Lower the Bar (At First)**
   - People fail because they try to go from zero to extreme overnight.
   - Start stupidly small. Five minutes. One rep. A single step.
   - Once you start, momentum takes over.
2. **Never Negotiate With Yourself**
   - Your brain will try to talk you out of things.
   - Ignore the debate. Just act.
   - Instead of thinking, *Should I go to the gym?*, just stand up and start moving.
3. **Show Up Every Single Day**
   - Even if it's just five minutes—show up.
   - Consistency beats intensity every time.

   Discipline means showing up, no matter what. Even when you're tired. Even when you're unmotivated. Even when everything in you wants to quit—you do it anyway. That's what separates the successful from the ones who never move forward.
4. **Make It Automatic**
   - Tie new habits to something you already do.

- Example: Do ten push-ups right after brushing your teeth.
- Example: Read for five minutes right after your morning coffee.

Discipline is not optional. You don't *try* to be disciplined. Either you are, or you aren't. Once again, the choice is yours. Train your mind to think: *This isn't a decision. It's a reflex. It's just what I **do.***

When you master discipline, you master life. Your results are a reflection of your habits. Winners don't rely on motivation—they rely on discipline. The ones who get results? They don't wait. They don't whine. They don't make excuses. What do they do? They show up. *Every. Damn. Day.*

Put This Into Action:
- Choose one small discipline to master. It could be making your bed, journaling, or doing a 5-minute workout. Start today.
- Create a no-excuses plan. What's one challenge that usually knocks you off track? How will you remain disciplined when it happens?
- Track your consistency. Use a notebook, app, or simple checkmarks on a calendar to see how often you follow through.

Reflection

- Where do you tend to rationalize your way out of action?
- What promise have you made to yourself that you keep breaking?
- What might change if you honored that promise today?

Core Message: WINNERS AREN'T MORE MOTIVATED—THEY'RE MORE DISCIPLINED.

5
Action Comes First

Success Isn't a One-Time Thing.

"For any movement to gain momentum, it must start with a small action."

Adam Braun

ONE action leads to the next. The hardest part is starting—but once you do, momentum carries you forward. Most people stop and start over and over. Winners keep the engine running. They keep making progress.

> An object at rest stays at rest, and an object in motion stays in motion with the same speed and in the same direction unless acted upon by an unbalanced force.
>
> – Isaac Newton

Newton wasn't only talking about physics. Your life works in much the same way: once you start moving, it's easier to keep going.

The first five seconds of a cold shower are brutal. Your body tenses, your breath shortens, and your mind screams at you to get out. But then something happens—you adapt. Your breathing steadies, your muscles relax, and you realize you can handle it. The discomfort doesn't disappear—you just become stronger than it. The fix? **Stop stopping.** Consistency is king.

Many people say, "If I can't do it perfectly, I might as well not do it at all." That's dead wrong. Action beats paralysis. Do something—anything—that moves you toward your objective, even if it seems insignificant.

Others believe every detail must be mapped out before they start. Also wrong. There's nothing wrong with planning—but don't get lost in the weeds. Sometimes, just knowing the destination is enough.

Some people say that missing a day here or there is no big deal. Well, it *can* be huge. Missing one day makes it easier to miss two. Then your momentum is at risk. And anything beyond two days? Momentum is dead. Now you're starting over.

Momentum is your greatest weapon. The people who get ahead aren't the smartest, strongest, or most talented—they're the ones who keep moving. Every time you push through imperfection, stay consistent, and act instead of waiting, you reinforce the habit of winning. Small actions add up. Tiny wins become unstoppable momentum. **Keep going.**

Momentum is a compounding force. Small actions stack up over time until progress feels inevitable. But it starts with lowering the activation energy. Make starting so easy it's almost stupid. Want to work out? Commit to just five minutes. Want to write? Open the document and type a single sentence. That's it. Getting started is the hard part—so trick yourself into motion.

Next, create a daily non-negotiable. One habit. Every single day. No excuses. It doesn't matter how small—one paragraph, one walk, one push-up. What matters is showing up. Keep the streak alive. Every day you check that box, you're proving to yourself that you're the kind of person who follows through.

Once you're consistent, **stack habits for maximum power**. Tie new habits to ones you're already doing. Drop down for ten push-ups right after brushing your teeth. Read for five minutes after your morning coffee. Link them together until momentum carries you forward without thinking.

The One Percent Rule is real. You don't need massive change. You need small, daily improvements. Just one percent better every day, and you're thirty-seven times better by year's end.

Compounding is the most powerful force there is. You won't see it instantly. But stick with it—and the results show up. **Always.**

Momentum is everything. Once you have it, guard it with your life. It's easier to keep moving than to start over. Consistency *trumps* intensity. Small wins daily beat random big efforts.

Put This Into Action:
- Start with a micro-win. What's one small thing you can complete right now that moves you forward? Do it immediately.
- Make a habit tracker. Pick one action (writing, exercise, etc.) and track how many days in a row you complete it.
- Embrace imperfection. If you miss a day, don't miss twice. Get back on track *right now*.

Reflection

- What's something important that you keep postponing?
- How could one small action break the inertia around it?
- How would it feel to be in motion—even before you feel motivated?

Core Message: SMALL, CONSISTENT ACTIONS CREATE UNSTOPPABLE MOMENTUM. KEEP MOVING, AND PROGRESS BECOMES INEVITABLE.

6
Stack Wins

Strong Minds Adapt and Overcome.

"The question isn't who is going to let me; it's who is going to stop me."

Ayn Rand, *The Fountainhead*

LIFE will punch you in the face. That's a guarantee. Most people crumble at the first sign of resistance. The winners? They take the hit, get back up, and keep swinging.

Pain is inevitable. Suffering is *optional.* Hard times are coming—that's not up for debate. You can't control what happens. But as Viktor Frankl taught us, you *can* control how you respond.

Example: Two people lose their jobs. One spirals into self-pity. The other sees it as an opportunity.

The fix? **Shift your perspective.** Hard times aren't roadblocks—they're training grounds.

Negative thoughts *will* come. That's a fact. The trick is stopping them before they control you.

How do you kill negative thoughts before they kill you? Use the **three-second rule**: The moment you catch a negative thought, give yourself three seconds. Replace it with an opposing, action-driven thought. *Move forward.* No dwelling. No overthinking.

Examples:
- "This is too hard." → "Hard is where the growth happens!"
- "Didn't get the job?" → "Rejection is just redirection!"
- "I'm not good enough." → "I'll get better with practice."

How to Build Mental Toughness (Even When You Feel Weak)

1. **Control What You Can. Ignore the Rest.**
   - Worrying about things outside your control is wasted time and energy.
   - Focus on actionable steps—not problems you can't fix.

2. **Seek Discomfort Intentionally.**
   - Comfort makes you soft. Challenge makes you strong.
   - Do one uncomfortable thing daily.
   - Examples: Cold showers, public speaking, difficult conversations.

3. **Develop a "So What?" Attitude.**
    - Life knocked you down? So what? Get back up.
    - Someone doubted you? So what? Prove them wrong.
    - You failed? So what? Learn and move forward.

Weak-minded people see failure as a dead end. Strong-minded people see failure as an educational experience.

Try this the next time you falter: Own it—no excuses, no blaming. Extract the lesson. Every failure has a takeaway. Adapt and go again. Fail fast. Learn fast. Do better.

Real growth is trying, failing, and adapting. Strength isn't built when life is easy—it's built when life is hard. You don't get tougher in comfort—you get tougher in the trenches. Challenges break most people. They don't have to break you. Develop an unshakable mind, and *nothing* will stop you.

Put This Into Action:
- Flip a negative thought. Catch yourself in self-doubt today. Reframe it into something constructive.
- Push through resistance. Find a task you've been avoiding. Take the first step—even if it's small.
- Celebrate resilience. Think of one moment when you overcame a mental roadblock. Use it as proof that you can do it again.

Reflection

- What are three small wins you've had recently?
- How do you typically celebrate progress (if at all)?
- Where can you create a quick win today?

Core Message: YOUR FUTURE DEPENDS ON THE WAY YOU SEE TODAY.

7
Persistence Over Perfection

Winning Isn't About Intensity. It's About Consistency.

"Success is the sum of small efforts, repeated day in and day out."

Robert Collier

WHEN it comes to achieving long-term success, there's one principle that rises above all others: **consistency**. No amount of motivation, talent, or resources can substitute for the relentless power of showing up and putting in the work, day after day. While effort may vary, consistency transforms effort into results.

Why is consistency so powerful? Because it compounds. Small, deliberate actions repeated over time lead to extraordinary outcomes. Think of a musician practicing scales, an athlete training daily, or an entrepreneur refining their craft. They may not see massive results in the short term, but the accumulated impact of consistent effort is undeniable. Success isn't about making one grand leap. It's about the small steps taken every day.

Consistency doesn't mean perfection. It's not about never making mistakes or always feeling on top of your game. It's about showing up—even when you don't feel like it. Missing one day doesn't matter much. What matters is not letting one missed day turn into two, three, or more. Excellence requires **persistence** more than perfection.

Here are a few practical tips for staying consistent:

1. **Focus on small wins.** Break down your goals into smaller, actionable steps. Small victories are easier to achieve, and each one builds momentum for the next.
2. **Create a routine.** Habits thrive in a structured environment. Set a schedule for your work, fitness, or personal goals and make it a non-negotiable part of your day.
3. **Track your progress.** Use a journal, app, or chart to record your efforts. Seeing progress visually is motivating and keeps you accountable.
4. **Embrace accountability.** Share your goals with someone who will hold you to your commitments. Sometimes, external encouragement can make all the difference.

Consider the story of an author who wrote one page a day. At first, it felt insignificant—even frustrating. But over a year, those daily pages added up to a 365-page manuscript. The same applies to fitness: doing ten push-ups a day might not feel transformative, but over time, the strength you build becomes undeniable.

Think about your own goals. What small, consistent actions can you commit to? Maybe it's reading 10 pages of a book daily, taking a 20-minute walk, or spending 15 minutes brainstorming ideas. These actions may seem trivial, but their cumulative effect is powerful.

What happens when life throws obstacles in your way? The key is **adaptability**. If your routine gets disrupted, find ways to adjust rather than abandon your goals entirely. Consistency doesn't mean rigidity—it means persistence despite challenges. Keep a "minimum effort" plan in your pocket for days when something unexpected comes up. That way, you can still make progress—even if it's small.

Consistency builds trust in both yourself and your abilities. Each time you follow through on a commitment, you reinforce the belief that you're capable of achieving what you set out to do. This self-trust becomes a foundation for confidence and further success.

Ultimately, consistency doesn't just lead to results—it shapes your identity. You become someone who takes action, who shows up, who follows through. And that's the person who achieves long-term success.

Most people can go hard for a little while. The ones who actually change their lives? They stay in the game when everyone else quits. This isn't about a phase—it's about a permanent upgrade.

The biggest mistake people make is sprinting when they should be pacing. Too many people start strong but burn out fast.

They go all-in for a month, then crash and burn. The fix? Think long-term. Pace yourself. **Make this a lifestyle.**

Willpower is overrated. It fades. Systems are reliable. They keep you dialed in when willpower fails.

How to Build Systems That Work:
1. **Schedule It**—If it's not on your calendar, it may not happen.
2. **Automate Decisions**—Make choices in advance, so you don't have to think about them later.
3. **Create Triggers**—Tie your habits to existing ones. Example: Read 10 pages after your morning coffee.

Learn to love boring work. Success isn't glamorous—it's about doing the boring stuff consistently well. Champions master the basics and repeat them daily. Exciting goals won't save you. *Your daily habits will.* The question isn't "Can I go hard today?" It's "Can I show up every day?"

Burnout is the silent killer of progress. If you go too hard, too fast, too often—you'll crash. The solution? Build in recovery days and cycles.

Sustainable Success Formula:
1. Push hard when needed.
2. Recover when needed.
3. Repeat Steps 1 & 2 as needed.

The people who succeed aren't the ones who never fall—they're the ones who never stay down. Build a life you don't need to escape from.

Sprints are temporary. Systems last forever. Focus on consistency—not perfection. **Don't let "perfect" demolish "good enough."**

What's one area of your life where you've struggled with consistency? Identify a small, actionable step you can start taking today. Remember: it's not about being perfect—it's about showing up. Because consistency truly is king.

Put This Into Action:
- Choose one habit and commit to it for seven days. Whether it's reading, writing, or exercising—stick with it for a full week.
- Make it non-negotiable. Treat your commitment like a meeting—schedule it and show up.
- Use "just 5 minutes" to get started. Feeling resistance? Tell yourself you'll just do five minutes. More often than not, you'll keep going.

Reflection

- Where has perfectionism slowed you down?
- What task could you complete imperfectly today—just to build momentum?
- What might be possible if progress mattered more than polish?

Core Message: STEADY EFFORT OVER TIME LEADS TO LASTING SUCCESS.

8
Don't Miss Twice

Build Your Future

"You may encounter many defeats, but you must not be defeated. In fact, it may be necessary to encounter the defeats, so you can know who you are, what you can rise from, how you can still come out of it."

Maya Angelou

W E'VE crushed excuses, built discipline, created momentum, and locked in long-term success. Now, there's only one thing left—**action**.

Because none of this matters if you don't do something with it. This final chapter is your blueprint. Your challenge. Your kick in the ass. No more waiting. No more planning. It's time to execute.

Reading this book won't change your life. Only your *action* will. Too many people read, get hyped—and do nothing.

You? You're different. Because you're going to act. You're going to win. You're going to win because of the knowledge you've gained. You're growing and improving every day. You're not the same person you were. Remember, it's not just what you know—it's how you *use* it.

The 30-Day Execution Plan: ONE MONTH. ONE FOCUS. MASSIVE CHANGE.

- **Week 1: Build Momentum.** Pick **ONE** key habit you want to install. Start small as hell. Just show up. Track it daily—**no missed days.**
- **Week 2: Push Through Resistance.** Double down—even when you don't feel like it. Cut out one major distraction holding you back. Keep stacking wins. Big or small, they all count.
- **Week 3: Increase the Challenge.** Raise the bar. Go harder. Go longer. Demand more from yourself. Review your progress—are you charging ahead or just coasting? Analyze, adjust, and attack.
- **Week 4: Lock It in *Forever*.** Turn your habit into a **system**. Systems are your secret sauce. They're your ticket to a better you. Build a long-term plan—this isn't a phase. Start thinking bigger.

No one's coming to save you. But **YOU**? You can save yourself. You **WILL** save yourself—because you believe in your own potential.

Truth Bomb: You either do it, or not. There's nothing left to say. No more tips, strategies, or life hacks. They're all worthless without action. You know what to do. The only question is: **Will you?**

Final Takeaway: This is your defining moment. You have everything you need—now *use* it. No more hesitation. No more delays. Just action. You control your destiny. Your time is now. *ROLL.*

Put This Into Action:
- Write down your top three priorities. What matters most right now? Be specific.
- Break them into steps. What's the first action you can take toward each one? Do every one *today*.
- Find an accountability partner. Share your commitment with someone who will hold you to it.

Your No Excuses
Total Commitment Contract

Write this down. *Sign* it. *Commit* to it.

I _____ commit to:

1. Taking action daily toward my personal and professional growth—no matter how small.
2. Not waiting for motivation—just doing the work.
3. Refusing to let excuses win.
4. Becoming the person I know I can be.

Signature: _____

Reflection

- Think of a recent slip-up. How did you respond?
- What does it mean to you to miss once—but not twice?
- What's one way to bounce back without shame?

Core Message: THIS ONE? WRITE IT YOURSELF—WITH *YOUR* ACTIONS.

Afterword

"I have been impressed with the urgency of doing. Knowing is not enough; we must apply. Being willing is not enough; we must do."

Leonardo da Vinci

CONGRATULATIONS —you've made it to the end of *Unstuck: Brutal Guidance for Getting Out of Your Own Way.* This is not just the conclusion of a book—it's the beginning of your transformation. The road ahead will be marked by challenges. There will be both victories and defeats. You now know how to handle either situation with skill and grace. This new perspective will be your steadfast partner along the way.

Throughout this book, the author has explored Stoic principles without explicitly naming them. Stoicism—a philosophy founded in ancient Greece by Zeno of Citium and later refined by Roman thinkers like Seneca, Epictetus, and Marcus Aurelius—offers a timeless framework for living a fulfilling life.

At its core, Stoicism emphasizes four cardinal virtues: **wisdom, courage, justice, and temperance**. These virtues serve as guiding principles, helping you cultivate resilience, clarity, and ethical behavior as you move through life.

Wisdom is the ability to discern what is true, useful, and meaningful. In Stoicism, wisdom isn't just about acquiring knowledge—it's about applying it effectively. A wise person distinguishes between what they can and cannot control, focusing their efforts on the former while accepting the latter with grace.

Courage is not merely physical bravery but also moral fortitude. It's the willingness to face difficulty, pain, or fear without compromising your principles. Courage allows you to endure hardship, speak the truth even when it's unpopular, and persist in the pursuit of virtue despite obstacles.

Justice governs your interactions with others. It's not merely about obeying laws—it's about upholding fairness, integrity, and compassion. It requires you to conduct yourself in ways that contribute to the well-being of others, ensuring that you neither harm nor tolerate harm.

Temperance is the virtue of self-discipline, balance, and moderation. It's about regulating desires and emotions so you're not controlled by excess or indulgence. Temperance allows you to enjoy life's pleasures in a measured way, without being enslaved by them.

These four virtues form a complete framework for living your best life. They align perfectly with this book's core message of taking responsibility, acting with intention, and forging a path toward lasting personal growth. Wisdom helps you make sound decisions. Courage empowers you to do what's right, even when it's hard. Justice guides how you treat others. Temperance ensures that consistency—not fleeting emotion—drives your choices.

Now that you've absorbed the principles outlined in this book, the real work begins. Success isn't about grand, sweeping gestures. It's the accumulation of small, deliberate actions taken daily. There will be days when all you can do is show up. That, too, is an act of courage.

Embrace each moment as an opportunity to refine yourself. Every choice you make brings you closer to the person you aspire to become. With the ideas in this book as your foundation, you have everything you need to construct a life of purpose, resilience, and fulfillment.

If this book resonated with you, I encourage you to engage further—growth thrives in community, and sharing your insights strengthens both your journey and others'.
1. **Visit my website:** `PRHuffman.ghost.io` — Get more advice, updates, and insights for living your best life.
2. **Join the conversation:** Connect with others on similar paths. Share your journey and learn from theirs.
3. **Spread the word:** Recommend this book to a friend, relative, or colleague who might benefit from its message.

About the Author

I want you to wake up and take control of your life–because no one else is going to do it for you. My own life was a disaster until I realized I could–and should–do more. *Unstuck: Brutal Guidance for Getting Out of Your Own Way* is a compilation of hard-earned lessons from my therapist Kelci, years of relentless reading, and the long, slow, messy low crawl towards growth.

For most of my adult life, I struggled with Major Depressive Disorder, compounded by undiagnosed ADHD–Inattentive Type. That cocktail fueled a continuous cycle of underper-  formance and self-doubt leaving me stuck and frustrated.

A great deal has changed since Kelci introduced me to Acceptance and Commitment Therapy (ACT). That's when things began–slowly, at first–to click. I was waiting to feel better before I did something. Where actually, I needed to do something to feel better. That shift in perspective changed everything.

At my core, I believe relentless self-education is the key to a better life. "Learn," I say. "Learn about the arts. Learn about science. Learn about history. And above all, learn about yourself—and be ready to get brutally honest in the process." Kelci remains a huge influence in my life because she helped me see what I couldn't: the greatest force holding me back was myself.

I read constantly. I'm drawn to thinkers who challenge conventional wisdom and widen the lens on what's possible. Carl Sagan's works especially *Cosmos*, *Pale Blue Dot*, and *The Demon-Haunted World*—formed how I think about science, reason, and our place in the universe. His writing reminds me that we are capable of so much more than we know—but only if we choose to step up.

These days, happiness means facing the mirror without self-loathing. It means no longer hiding from hard truths or waiting for life to magically improve. It means owning every step—especially the ugly ones—and walking forward anyway.

As I wrote *Unstuck*, I kept thinking about a younger version of myself: a man with no clear direction, focused outward, waiting for a break that never came. If that's where you are right now, hear me: waiting is a losing strategy. You can live a different, better life—and I'm living proof of that.

My mission is simple: help you break free, take control of your life, and get yourself unstuck.

From the Author

A Personal Note from the Author

The following essay offers a more personal glimpse into the mindset and experience that shaped *Unstuck*. In my own words, I reflect on what it truly means to get unstuck—and why this book had to be written.

I didn't set out to write a book. I set out to save myself.

There was a long, insufferable stretch of my life where everything felt heavy. Progress seemed impossible. I had ideas, intentions, even a vague sense of purpose–but nothing moved. I was stuck. Not usually in the dramatic, fall-apart-at-the-seams way. More often it was like a slow erosion of clarity and will. The days blurred. The excuses multiplied. And the longer I waited for change, the further away it seemed.

I knew what I should be doing. But knowing isn't doing. And I had spent too much time collecting insights without ever applying them. My bookshelf was full, and my soul was empty.

Eventually, I stopped looking for the perfect system or secret formula and asked a harder question: What's the smallest action I'm willing to take *today*?

That question changed everything. Because the answer was almost always *something*. And *action*—no matter how small—is the enemy of stuck.

I started building momentum in the only way that matters: by doing. Writing. Moving. Cleaning. Creating. I wasn't chasing motivation anymore. I was building it—one small act of discipline at a time.

This book came out of that process. It was never meant to be perfect—it was meant to be useful. And it was never meant to sound like a sermon. It was meant to feel like a voice in your corner, reminding you that stuck isn't permanent. That motion creates clarity. That you don't need to fix everything—just the next thing.

So here it is. My experience, my lessons, my scars. If anything in these pages helps you get moving again, then every hour I spent writing was worth it.

Acknowledgments

WRITING this book has been an incredible journey—one that would not have been possible without the support, guidance, and encouragement of so many people.

First and foremost, I want to express my deepest gratitude to my former therapist, Kelci, who inspired me to write this book, and to the many friends who stood by me through the ups and downs of the process. Your unwavering support and belief in me fueled my determination to bring this project to life.

A special thanks goes to Chatty–my tireless collaborator, brainstorming partner, and LLM. Her ideas for restructuring chapters, along with meticulous proofreading, were invaluable in shaping the message of this book.

To all the mentors, authors, and thinkers who've influenced my perspective—thank you for providing the wisdom and insight that helped me articulate my thoughts with clarity and conviction.

My heartfelt gratitude goes to all the fine people working at the Veterans Administration's Kansas City Medical Center. I doubt I'd be doing anything today without them. They are an incredible team of professionals. There are far too many to name here, but you know who you are.

And finally—to you, the reader. Your willingness to challenge yourself, lean into discomfort, seek growth, and take action is what makes this book truly come alive. I wrote this for you. I hope it serves as the wake-up call you've been waiting for—the one that helps you move forward and make real change.

Thank you *all*.

Key Principles

These aren't steps to follow blindly—they're reminders to return to when you feel stuck, tired, or tempted to wait for "someday."

1. You don't need more time—you need to start. Clarity comes from action, not the other way around.
2. Discipline isn't punishment—it's self-respect in motion. You act not because it's easy, but because you said you would.
3. Start small. Stay consistent. Momentum doesn't come from occasional effort—it comes from continuous motion.
4. Your excuses are loud, but they aren't final. You get to choose what you do next. Always.
5. Progress is not perfection. Forward is forward, no matter how slow.
6. Getting unstuck is not a single decision. It's a thousand micro-decisions made on hard days when no one is watching.
7. You already have what you need to begin. Waiting for more just postpones what you're capable of today.

Reading List

These books have shaped, challenged, or sharpened my thinking. Some align closely with the message of *Unstuck*. Others don't — and that's exactly why they're here. Growth comes not just from agreement, but from contrast and clarity.

Books That Reinforce the Core

- **Extreme Ownership** – Jocko Willink & Leif Babin
  A brutal, battlefield-tested case for total accountability — no excuses, ever.
- **The War of Art** – Steven Pressfield
  Resistance is real, and this book doesn't sugarcoat it. Art or action, the enemy is within.
- **Atomic Habits** – James Clear
  Clear thinking on small changes that create big shifts — no mysticism, just systems.
- **The Happiness Trap** – Russ Harris
  ACT stripped down and made useful. If

you want to suffer less without lying to yourself, start here.
- **Can't Hurt Me** – David Goggins
Raw, relentless, and uncomfortable in the best way. Goggins doesn't ask for pity—he demands action. A case study in radical accountability and the brutal edge of mental toughness.

Books That Push Back

- **The Gifts of Imperfection**–Brené Brown
Encourages you to embrace vulnerability and let go of who you think you're supposed to be. Valuable, but softer than my approach. I say don't just embrace your mess–*sort it out*.
- **A Return to Love** – Marianne Williamson
Spiritual, abstract, and heartfelt. But I believe transformation requires structure, not surrender.
- **The Alchemist** – Paulo Coelho
Inspires many. Didn't hit me that way. Following omens isn't my path–building discipline is.

Books That Ground Me

- **Man's Search for Meaning**—Viktor Frankl
A quiet, devastating reminder that meaning is possible even in the worst conditions–but it's our job to find it.

- **Meditations**—Marcus Aurelius
  Stoic clarity from a Roman emperor. Control what you can, endure what you must, and do what's right–no matter the mood.
- **Discipline Equals Freedom**—Jocko Willink
  Not a how-to—more of a field manual. Sparse, raw, and useful when your mind starts negotiating.
- **Make Your Bed**—Admiral William H. McRaven
  Simple truths from a man who's lived them. It's not just a metaphor–it's a habit worth keeping.

Though no single system owns these ideas, their presence is woven into every chapter.

30-Day Momentum Challenge

You don't need to overhaul your life in a weekend. What you need is consistent, imperfect motion. This challenge is designed to help you build that momentum—one decision at a time. Each day, complete the small action listed. Don't overthink it. Just show up.

- Week 1 — Start Moving
    1. Make your bed. Do it with intention.
    2. Identify one thing you've been avoiding. Take five minutes to face it.
    3. Write down three things you're grateful for.
    4. Declutter one small area:
        - a drawer
        - a desktop
        - a folder
    5. Take a 10-minute walk without your phone.
    6. Choose one thing to finish today. Finish it.

7. Reflect: What does the word "unstuck" mean to you?
- Week 2 — Build Discipline
    8. Wake up 15 minutes earlier. Use that time deliberately.
    9. Do something hard on purpose. Notice how it feels.
    10. Write for 10 minutes about what you want from these 30 days.
    11. Turn off all screens 30 minutes before bed.
    12. Cancel one commitment you no longer believe in.
    13. Say no to something—politely and firmly.
    14. Reflect: What's the difference between rest and avoidance?
- Week 3 — Strengthen Self-Respect
    15. Write down one core value. Take at least one action aligned with it today.
    16. Reach out to someone you've lost touch with.
    17. Move your body for 20 minutes—walk, stretch, lift, dance.
    18. Identify one excuse you've been telling yourself. Challenge it.
    19. Finish something you've been putting off.
    20. Practice doing one task with full attention—no multitasking.
    21. Reflect: How have your actions shaped your self-image?

- Week 4 — Sustain Momentum
  22. Say out loud one goal you've been afraid to name.
  23. Set a timer for 25 minutes and do focused work on one task.
  24. Do one thing today that future-you will thank you for.
  25. Revisit a previous day's action and do it again—better.
  26. Let go of something: an object, an expectation, a story.
  27. Do something creative—just for the joy of it.
  28. Reflect: Where do you feel stuck right now? What's one step forward? Take it.
- Final Two Days — Own It
  29. Review the past 28 days. What changed? What didn't?
  30. Write a one-sentence commitment to yourself—and keep it visible.

Prompts for Chapter Illustrations

1. **At the Crossroads** An oil painting of a solitary figure standing at a fork in a shadowy path, bathed in a warm glow ahead. A faint, ghostly clock hangs in the night sky above. The mood is contemplative and symbolic, representing decision and the passage of time.
2. **Shadows of the Mind** A seated man in a dim room rests his head on one hand, lost in thought. Behind him on the wall, shadowy, monstrous figures loom, representing internal struggles. A window to the right reveals a bright, calm landscape, suggesting the possibility of peace beyond turmoil.
3. **The Scars We Carry** A muscular, scarred figure stands with his back to the viewer, facing a post-apocalyptic wasteland at dusk. The sky is tinged with fire, and his scars are pronounced. It symbolizes resilience, survival, and strength earned through adversity.

4. **Starstuff** A solitary figure stands on a hill, gazing at a star-filled night sky. A faint face—perhaps a memory or cosmic vision—emerges in the stars. The tone is reverent and reflective, evoking Carl Sagan's concept that we are all made of starstuff.
5. **The Long Road** A massive round stone sits in the foreground of a winding dirt path that snakes into golden hills. The landscape is warmly lit under a wide, open sky. It symbolizes effort, persistence, and the journey ahead.
6. **The Climb** A lone figure climbs a staircase, burdened by a heavy golden sphere on his back. The background is a glowing mix of warm yellows and soft blues. It conveys the struggle and determination of carrying purpose upward.
7. **Through the Gauntlet** A man walks confidently down a narrow corridor bathed in golden light. On either side, tall shadowy figures appear but do not impede him. The tone is resolute and bright, representing courage and self-belief.
8. **Away from the Wreckage.** A solitary figure walks away from the wreckage of a collapsed structure, moving steadily toward the light.

Afterword. The Craftsman A weathered artisan carefully chisels a sculpture from a block of wood in a warmly lit workshop. His tools are scattered, and his concentration is intense. The image honors slow, focused work and personal mastery.

Notes

www.ingramcontent.com/pod-product-compliance
Lightning Source LLC
Chambersburg PA
CBHW050523100526
44581CB00005B/115